To *Jacob*

We are so excited about your many explorations to come, Jacob!
You can seek adventures in this giant country,
from the West Coast to the east, all the marvels in between,
and the beauty of the north. You are truly a Canadian kid,
so enjoy learning and celebrating this rich culture.

Love, *Grandma*

A note to you, dear *reader*,

Canada is a huge land, part of North America. This continent has been known by many of the original peoples as Turtle Island. It actually is shaped like a turtle! Indigenous children played on this land long before it was known as Canada. The First Nations people, Métis Nations, and Inuit lived in respect of the land. Others came from Europe, colonizing the country and giving it the current name of Canada. People continue to move to Canada from around the world, and add to its cultural richness. The hope is that newcomers and original people can live in respect of each other and of the land, and learn from each other. May the children reading this book also feel this love of the land, people and diverse culture.

Hi! Bonjour!

I am *Jacob.*

We have a big country to explore, but let's do our best to at least see a little of each province and territory. I have a map at the end of this book so you can see where we go, remember some of the fun stuff we do or see, or yummy foods we try! I wonder which part of Canada you will like the most? Oh, and I'm bringing Hockey Stick Buddy with me, so see if you can find it in each scene! And watch for the Canadian flag!

CANADA

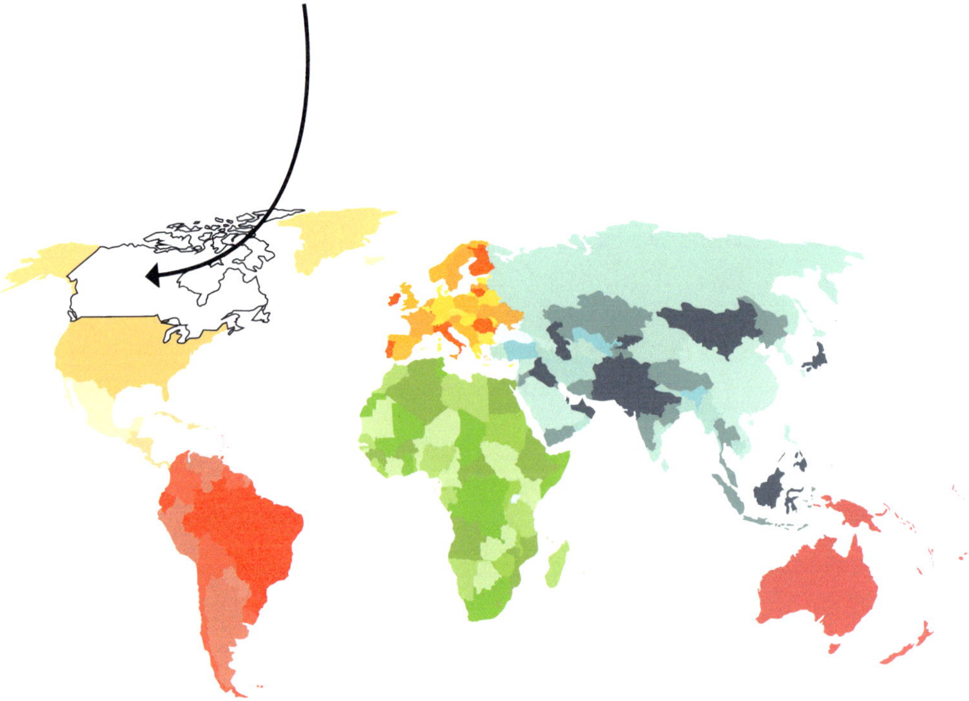

Here is Canada, in North America. The furthest west is Vancouver Island on the Pacific Ocean, and the country stretches eastward to the Atlantic Ocean. The cold Arctic Ocean is at the north, and the United States of America falls along the southern border. It will be fun to stop in each province and territory as we learn about this very big country! You can look at where we've been at the end of our travels!

If we start from the west, Vancouver Island comes first
As we travel this huge northern land.
I've seen the regal and rugged both on the island.
Now I've ferried across to the mainland.

Let's visit Vancouver's Stanley Park.
Try some smoked candied salmon and now…
We journey to sunshine then down to the lakes.
Let's pick some fresh fruit! Oh wow!

The area along the west coast is known by many as the Sunshine Coast, but it actually gets a lot of rain. Some parts are even rainforests!
The Okanagan area of BC is popular for summer vacations, with warm weather, delicious fruit, and lakes.
OKANAGAN

The Calgary Stampede is the largest outdoor rodeo in the world.
There is a giant decorated egg statue, or 'pysanka' in Vegreville, celebrating Ukrainian heritage.

Wow! It seems all is big in Alberta.
A dinosaur, an egg and a tipi!
I went flying on rides in Edmonton's mall,
And I sailed down huge mountains on skis!

Driving east through Saskatchewan's big skies,
Waving to fields of canola and wheat.
Play ball and learn how to curl now.
Then Saskatoon berry pie to eat!

There are thousands of lakes in Manitoba.
Hey! Let's fish, swim and canoe!
In winter we can cheer on the dog sleds.
I've never seen a polar bear! Have you?

The maple leaf symbol is on the Canadian flag. Certain maple trees give the sap for delicious maple syrup!

Toronto has three major league sports teams: Basketball, hockey and baseball!

Visit museums and cheer on teams in Toronto.
Then go boating on the Great Lakes, so pretty.
Now tour Parliament Buildings and monuments
In Ottawa, Canada's capital city.

Let's head to Québec now. "Allons-y."
Say "Bonjour" to Bonhomme at Carnaval!
Gobble delicious poutine, pea soup, and sugar pie
In Québec City's historic old walls.

There's much to see in this huge province.
Hike the shores of the Gaspésie.
On to Montréal's museums, cathedrals and more.
And while here we can watch hockey!

Now we are on to the Atlantic provinces.
New Brunswick is our first stop.
Step back in time at the Acadian Village,
Then run around at Hopewell Rocks!

Cross the Confederation Bridge to PEI now,
Then let's search for sea glass in the sand.
We dig potatoes from red earth for dinner,
Then learn of the fables of Anne.

From Halifax harbour to Cape Breton's park.
Look! The Bluenose is in Lunenburg's waters!
Holding on to my Sou'wester by Peggy's Cove lighthouse.
Now gobbling my dinner with lobster!

All of the Atlantic provinces are known for their seafood, including lobsters.

Newfoundland and Labrador, amazing lands to the east.
Hey look! Moose, puffins, icebergs and whales.
The history's rich culture includes Vikings,
And there's a lighthouse with a transatlantic tale.

The Beothuk people are lost, though other Indigenous tribes continue. Settlers sailed here from Ireland, as well as England and France. Even Vikings once lived here!

Wild salmon and berries, mystical lights.
Learn northern legends and tales, everyone!
Let's explore the Yukon Territory's amazing sights.
This land of the midnight sun.

Drive ice roads, strap on snowshoes, learn beadwork too.
Look! Muskox, whales and reindeer!
We paddle through canyons, fish on water or ice.
It really is exciting to explore here!

Nunavut's people live very far north.
Let's dress up warm and wrap food we are bringing
To feast on bannock and jam as we listen
To a duet of Inuit throat singing.

We are leaving the north, we had fun and learned much.
I love the squeak and the crunch of the snow.
Some parts are the furthest north on the Earth.
Watch their magic skies swirl as we go.

We’ve seen a little of each part of Canada.
We’ve met people, seen icebergs and moose.
I played hockey on so many ice rinks.
Now fly home like the Canada goose!

We geese are big. We traditionally migrate south in winter as a well-organized flock. We even take turns leading.

Here's a simple, delicious bread that has been made in Canada for over 200 years. The Scottish brought this recipe to North America, and it has been embraced by, and become part of the food culture by Indigenous peoples. Bannock or "fry bread" is enjoyed by all.

Bannock

WHAT YOU NEED

2 1/2 c flour (traditionally white but you can mix with whole wheat)
1 Tbsp baking powder
1/4 c oil (canola or other)
1 1/4 c water

HOW TO MAKE IT

Heat oven to 375 F.
Mix flour and baking powder in a big bowl. Make a little indentation in the middle and pour in the oil and water.
Mix it up with a large spoon, fork, or your fingers.
Spread about 1/2 c flour onto a counter or table. Scoop the dough from the bowl onto the floured area.
Fold or knead the dough for a few minutes until it seems soft but not sticky.
Put the dough onto a baking sheet that is greased or with parchment paper. Make an oval or circle that is about 1 in (2 cm) thick.
Pop the cookie sheet into the oven for 20 minutes.
Cut it into enough pieces to share. Now you can add butter or jam!

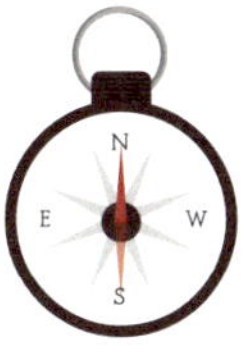

We made it all across Canada,
from the west to the east and the north!
Follow the numbers to see our journey!

LEGEND

1. British Columbia
2. Alberta
3. Saskatchewan
4. Manitoba
5. Ontario
6. Québec
7. New Brunswick
8. Prince Edward Island
9. Nova Scotia
10. Newfoundland & Labrador
11. Yukon
12. Northwest Territories
13. Nunavut

Here's your chance to colour!
You can look back in the book to see
these animals and more from
Jacob's visit to Canada.
You can colour them the same,
or use your imagination!
You can also colour Jacob and
Hockey Stick Buddy!

ABOUT THE AUTHOR

Candy

Candy loves kids' books, the sound of squeaky snow, and popcorn. She can't help reading books, especially if it lets her learn about people around the world. She read books to her little brother, then to her own kids, then to hundreds during her Library Programmer days. Now she reads to her grandkids. She even sends Grandma Videos to read to them from afar. Then, sometimes she just sits down and writes her own.

ABOUT THE DESIGNER

Jess

Jessica found her passion for drawing and designing at her grandparents house in Lima, Perú, where she would spend countless hours drawing and creating stories with her cousins. She loves art, reading, music, world history and culture, reading all kinds of books, and animals of all kinds. Her sons share her passion for animals and love to spoil their dog, Apollo.

Watch for other adventures as **Kids Visit the World.**
Next stop... **England with Alexa!**

And there are more friends and journeys to come!

Check out other books in our series:
Isabelle visits Perú
Sophie visits The Phillipines

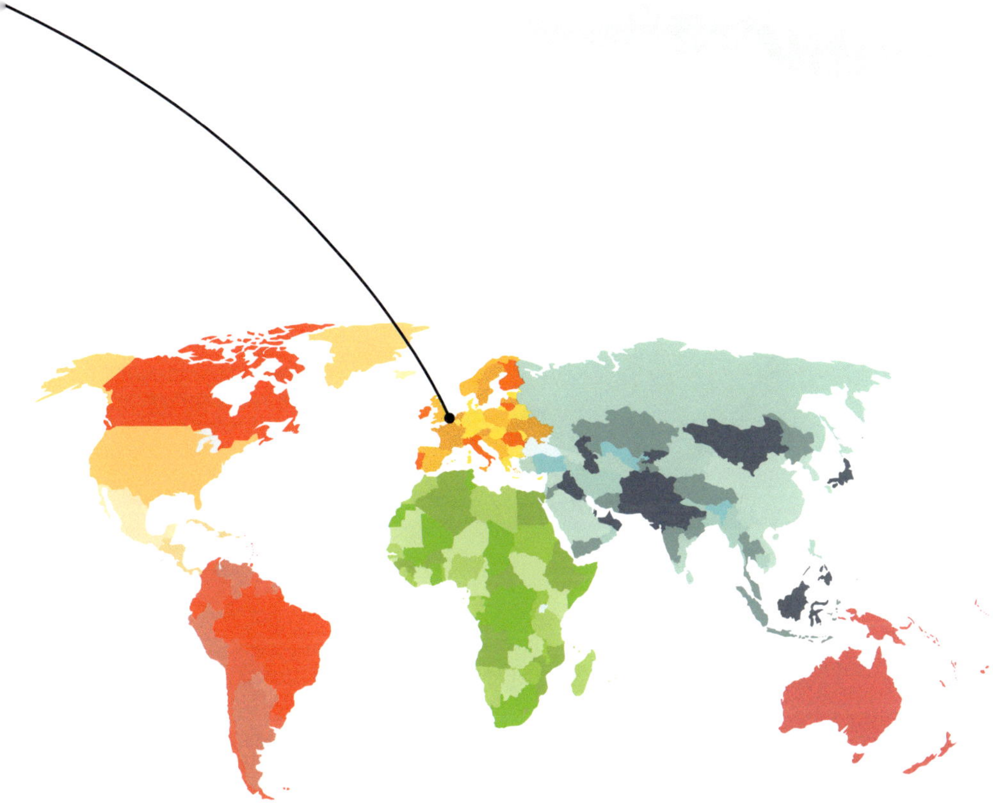

KIDS VISIT THE WORLD

EST 2024

@kids_visit_the_world

KidsVisitTheWorld@gmail.com

ISBN 978-0-9697032-3-5

Written by Candy Weisner
Designs by Jessica Ingard
Layout by J Bird Designs
Published by Thoughts For You
Made in Cochrane, Alberta, Canada

Made in United States
Troutdale, OR
06/25/2026

50361568R00024